# The F[illegible]t Quotes

## Humorous Quotations for All Sports Fans

James Conrad

Published by Blue Yonder Books

# Contents

# Introduction

**This is a book for those who love cricket and all that goes with it. Cricket is perhaps the most social of sports where cricketers can spend long periods together, sometimes days. There are few things that cricketers enjoy more than the mistakes of others. It is part of the enjoyment of cricket that these tales are shared with teammates and competitors.**

**This collection of quotes is essentially the mistakes, misspeaks and amusing observations of the great and the good of cricket.**

**The book is dedicated to all flannelled fools the world over.**

# The Love of the Game

**There is a widely held and quite erroneous belief that cricket is just another game.**
*The Duke of Edinburgh*

**Cricket is a game played by 11 fools and watched by 11,000 fools.**
*George Bernard Shaw*

**I want to play cricket, because I have found out that I am rubbish at everything else.**
*Stuart Law*

**Nothing happens in cricket, ever. Even the highlights resemble a freeze frame.**
*Charlie Brooker*

**Cricket requires one to assume such indecent postures.**
*Oscar Wilde*

**We don't play this game for fun.**
*Wilfred Rhodes*

**I think cricket is a boring game to watch.**
*Sunil Gavaskar*

**I don't have the patience for (golf). It's a long way to walk before you have a pint.**
*Colin Milburn*

**Sex is over and done with in a few moments unless you're Sting. Whereas a perfectly timed off drive for four lives on in the mind forever.**
*Marcus Berkmann, the author of Zimmer Men*

**Basically, it's just a whole bunch of blokes standing around scratching themselves.**
*Kathy Lette, Australian author*

**Whoever hoped like a cricketer?**
*R.C. Robertson-Glasgow*

**Say, when do they begin?**
*Groucho Marx at Lords*

**Admitting to being a Tory in Scotland is seen as weird, lie cross-dressing or liking cricket.**
*Fraser Nelson, the editor of the Spectator*

**Baseball has the great advantage over cricket of being ended sooner.**
*George Bernard Shaw*

**And I don't watch cricket. How can you like a game that requires you to take four days off work to follow a Test?**
*Thierry Henry*

**It's been a very slow and dull day, but it hasn't been boring. It's been a good, entertaining days cricket.**
*Tony Benneworth, ABC radio*

**Cricket civilizes people and creates good gentlemen. I want everyone to play cricket in Zimbabwe. I want ours to be a nation of gentlemen**
*Robert Mugabe*

**There may not be any attacks tonight because we are also watching the match.**
*A Tamil Tigers spokesman on halting fighting for the Sri Lanka's semi against New Zealand*

**Cricket is basically baseball on vallium.**
*Robin Williams*

**I'm confident they play the game in haven. Wouldn't be heaven otherwise would it?**
*Patrick Moore*

**It's a funny kind of month, October. For the really keen cricket fan, it's when you realise that your wife left you in May.**
*Dennis Norden*

**Cricket needs brightening up a bit. My solution is to let the players drink at the beginning of the game, not after. It always works in our picnic matches.**
*Paul Hogan*

**We did give him three initials because we thought it would look good on a scoresheet.**
*Chris Broad on son Stuart*

**Cricket is a game that lends itself very well to periods of introspection, particularly if you are a batsman and you get out early on in the innings. Then you have to just sit and watch others for a considerable amount of time.**
*Abhishek Ratna*

**A great advert for cricket.**
*Mark Lawrenson after watching a dire FA Cup final, being played just up the road from England's tussle with West Indies*

**Oh God. If there be cricket in heaven, let there also be rain.**
*Alec Douglas-Home*

**If I knew I was going to die today I would still want to know the cricket scores.**
*JH Hardy*

**Cricket makes no sense to me. I find it beautiful to watch and I like that they break for tea.**
*Jim Jarmusch, American film director*

**Many continentals think life is a game, the English think cricket is a game.**
*George Mikes, How to be an Alien in England*

**It was raining men. I thought I was dreaming. I was almost tempted to ask for a date.**
*Lisa Morrison on seeing a team of RAF parachutists, who missed their display at the cricket ground and landed in local gardens*

**I am hippopotamously happy and elephantastically proud.**
*Wes Hall on being honoured after his 70th birthday*

**You know that summer has arrived when you hear the sound of leather on Brian Close.**
*Eric Morecambe*

**Of all the races in the Galaxy, only the English could possibly revive the memory of the most horrific wars ever to sunder the Universe and transform it into what I'm afraid is generally regarded as an incomprehensibly dull and pointless game.**
*Douglas Adams, Life the Universe and Everything*

**I remember going for a drink with a friend once and being asked to talk about anything other than cricket for five minutes. We stayed silent until five minutes had passed, and then got back to cricket.**
*Chris Tavare*

**It's kind of hard to go on one date, have a nice dinner and then say: 'That was nice - what are you doing in six weeks' time? I'm going to Chittagong.'**
*Graeme Smith in Cape Times discussing dating problems*

# The Umpires

**It is rather suitable for umpires to dress like dentists, since one of their tasks is to draw stumps.**
*John Arlott*

**This idea that umpires are always right is a load of old cobblers. What I want to know is: Who umpires the umpires?**
*Geoff Boycott*

**The breeze is getting up and we can just about see Umpire Shepherd's trousers filling up with wind.**
*Jonathan Agnew*

**The modern umpire is caught between two opposing forces – the domestic pressure which encourage error and the technology which reveals them.**
*Imran Khan*

**I've only been in the match referee's room once and that was for wearing the wrong-coloured undergarment. It's ridiculous.**
*Stuart Broad*

**The only good thing about that decision, Gatt, is that I'll get tea before you.**
*Graham Gooch*

**There's no additives when you see me, no preservatives. It's freshly squeezed. What you see is what you get.**
*Billy Bowden*

**The third umpires should be changed as often as nappies... and for the same reason.**
*Navjot Sidhu*

**There's only one man made more appeals than you, George, and that was Dr Barnardo.**
*Umpire Bill Reeve to George MacAuley*

**Umpire Fenwick just itches his nose, rather than putting his finger up in the usual fashion.**
*Paul Allott*

**Too high? If the ball had hit his head it would have hit the bloody wickets.**
*Alan Brown, questioning an LBW appeal decision against 5ft 3in Harry Pilling*

**Man, haven't you heard of Mr Dickie Bird. This is one of his hats. I took it off his head at the World Cup final... we all ran onto the field and I won the race.**
*A bus conductor when Dickie Bird asked him where he got his hat from*

**We were disappointed, but then Billy Bowden told us it was just cheese.**
*Dinesh Chandimal after a missile hit a Sri Lanka player*

**If you want an argument in favour of the review system, put Harper on the field; if you want an argument against the system, put Harper in the third umpire's booth.**
*Simon Barnes is not a fan of Daryl Harper*

**If the umpire is as deaf as a post and as blind as a bat at least it's the same for both sides.**
*Giles Clarke*

**Life without sports is like life without underpants.**
*Billy Bowden*

# CRICKET MATHS

**A very small crowd here today. I can count the people on one hand, can't be more than 30.**
*Michael Abrahamson*

**Bill (Frindall) needs a small ruler. How about the Sultan of Brunei? I hear he is only four foot ten.**
*Brian Johnston*

**And we don't need a calculator to tell us that the required run-rate is 4.5454 per over.**
*Christopher Martin-Jenkins*

**It's a catch 21 situation.**
*Kevin Pietersen*

**Laird has been brought in to stand in the corner of the circle.**
*Richie Benaud*

**The Port Elizabeth ground is more of a circle than an oval. It is long and square.**
*Trevor Bailey*

**As my mates told me, that's the first hundred I've scored on TV for a while**
*Alastair Cook after beating James Anderson at darts*

**Statistics are like miniskirts; they reveal more than what they hide.**
*Navjot Singh Sidhu*

**The Port Elizabeth ground is more of a circle than an oval. It is long and square.**
*Trevor Bailey*

**Sri Lankan score is running like an Indian taximeter.**
*Navjot Singh Sidhu*

**Bill Frindall has done a bit of mental arithmetic with a calculator**
*John Arlott*

**The rest is not only history but will remain history for many years to come.**
*Jack Bannister*

**They say that a martini is like a woman's breast. One ain't enough and three is too many.**
*Chris Gayle*

**In terms of women's cricket in Bermuda, it has come a long way, but we still have a long way to go.**

*Bermuda captain Linda Mienzer putting a positive spin on the numbers. Her side was bowled out for 13 and South Africa chased the total in four balls at the ICC Women's World Cup Qualifier*

**An agent? That sounds suspiciously like something someone who actually earned money from the sport would have!**

*Claire Taylor, England batsman, wonders why she needs an agent*

# THE ART OF CAPTAINCY

**A well-trained collie dog could captain a cricket team.**
*Bill 'Tiger' O'Reilly*

**Ian Botham is in no way inhibited by a capacity to over-intellectualise.**
*Frances Edmonds*

**It was a good toss to lose and unfortunately, I won it**
*Kane Williamson*

**Playing against a team with Ian Chappell as a captain turns cricket match into gang warfare.**
*Mike Brearley*

**Most Pakistani sides have one unifying factor – they all hate the Captain**
*Simon Barnes*

**A captain cannot make a bad side into a good one, but a great side can make an indifferent captain into a moderate one.**
*Douglas Jardine*

**There were times when Closey could make Walter Mitty appear a modest realist.**
*Ray East on Brian Close*

**I presented my trousers to the Committee. I had nothing to hide**
*Michael Atherton after the dirt in trousers affair*

**I learnt a lot about captaincy by being told that I was an idiot.**
*Ian Chappell*

**Before the game we said, 'Let's make history today.' Well, we made history.**
*Dutch captain Luuk van Troost on Herschelle Gibbs's six sixes against them.*

**What can you say? I told Daan after the third ball, 'try to bowl a quicker one' and he said, 'I just did'.**
*Luuk van Troost after Herschelle Gibbs's onslaught against Daan van Bunge*

**The only difference with Gooch's tour and what happened on the Bounty was that Captain Bligh got that bit more support.**
*Greg Chappell*

**The best way to lead your side is with 500 runs behind you.**
*Graham Gooch*

**We've won one on the trot.**
*Alec Stewart*

**As harrowing occupations go, there can't be much to choose between the Australian cricket captaincy and social work on Skid Row.**
*Doug Ibbotson*

**The hallmark of a great captain is the ability to win the toss, at the right time.**
*Richie Benaud*

**We need good captains. We're pretty mediocre.**
*Jeremy Coney bids farewell to Stephen Fleming with a downbeat assessment of New Zealand cricket*

**Illy (Ray Illingworth) had the man-management skills of Basil Fawlty.**
*Darren Gough*

**He treated a one-day match as a practice match.**
*Ravi Shastri to Sunil Gavaskar. Gavaskar scored 36 not out off 136 balls chasing an England total of 335 in 60 overs in 1975*

**We know you can lose wickets in clusters and we seem to have lost 10 in a cluster.**
*Alastair Cook*

**I asked Jim Laker whether he felt we should bat or insert the opponents. He went out to have a look and was missing for a very long time. I asked Jim where he had been and he said he had been looking for the pitch and was still not sure he had found it.**
*Trevor Bailey*

**Graeme Swann the captain would never pick Graeme Swann the kid.**
*Graeme Swann, spells out his selection policy*

# Philosophy

**There is no such thing as a crisis in cricket, only the next ball.**
*WG Grace*

**Their unpredictability is not a challenge because they are predictably unpredictable. Their strength lies in the predictability of their unpredictability.**
*Russell Domingo sums up the Pakistan cricket team*

**If it's difficult, I'll do it now. If it's impossible, I'll do it presently.**
*Don Bradman*

**Experience is like a comb that life gives you when you are bald.**
*Navjot Singh Sidhu*

**Some days you are the windscreen, some you're the bug.**
*Michael Hussey*

**I would prefer to tell a young player what to do than how to do it.**
*Greg Chappell*

**A man with a music hall imagination.**
*John Arlott on Brian Johnston*

**That's what cricket's all about: two batsmen pitting their wits against one another**
*Fred Trueman*

**Baseball and cricket are beautiful and highly stylized medieval war substitutes, chess made flesh, a mixture of proud chivalry and base - in both senses - greed.**
*John Fowles*

**The Indians are finding the gaps like a pin a haystack.**
*Navjot Singh Sidhu*

**It's pretty simple stuff, but the complicated thing is to keep it simple.**
*Glenn McGrath*

**I don't really see myself as a cricketer. I see myself as quite a cultured person.**
*Adam Zampa*

**When you go to your grave, people will remember what you did with your life rather than how much money you made.**
*Justin Langer explaining why he's opting out of the IPL*

**Far from marking the end of nationalism, the IPL is the ultimate triumph of that principle: a global tournament in which the same nation always wins.**
*Gideon Haigh*

**Some are born with silver spoons in their mouths. I was born in Pudsey. You can't be luckier than that if you want to play cricket.**
*Ray Illingworth*

**Cricket speaks in languages far beyond that of politicians.**
*Nelson Mandela*

**An optimist sees the doughnut; the pessimist sees the hole.**
*Navjot Singh Sidhu*

**There's no sitting duck like a scared duck.**
*Ray Lindwall*

**Being manager of a touring team is rather like being in charge of a cemetery – lots of people underneath you, but no one is listening.**
*Wes Hall*

**Who made them boring?"**
*Richie Benaud responds to Geoff Boycott's call for four-day Tests because five days are, apparently, boring*

**Everyone keeps saying 'you'll know when it's time'. Well, at one o'clock two days ago I knew it was time - it just came to me.**
*Justin Langer talks about retirement from Test cricket*

**You have to try and reply to criticism with your intellect, not your ego.**
*Mike Brearley*

**It smells a lot different.**
*Sarah Taylor on being asked the difference between a male and female changing room*

**Never enough. Whatever it is in life, never enough.**
*Shane Warne*

**A Test match is like a painting. A one day game is like a Rolf Harris painting.**
*Ian Chappell*

**Taking it from behind**
*Richard Blakey's autobiography*

**One day cricket is like fast food. No one wants to cook.**
*Viv Richards*

# TACTICS

**We're happy to tootle along in a two litre diesel in a Formula 1 race.**

*Graeme Swann on England's one day tactics in 2014*

**I think the batsman's strategy will be to make runs and not get out.**

*Richie Benaud*

**I have prepared for the worst-case scenario, but it could be even worse than that.**

*Monty Panesar*

**My tactic would be to take a quick single and observe him from the other end.**

*Geoffrey Boycott's on playing Shane Warne.*

**You don't come to a cricket ground to draw a cricket match.**

*Ravi Shastri*

**The aim of English cricket is, in fact, mainly to beat Australia.**

*Jim Laker*

**You've only got to last two balls and then you will be fine.**

*Jimmy Cook to his son Stephen prior to his Test debut. Jimmy Cook was out first ball on his debut*

**They'd win the first four Tests and we'd try and nick one at the end when they were all drunk.**

*Nasser Hussain explaining Ashes tactics*

**If God can get me to 25, I can do the rest.**

*Derek Randall*

**Signing Kolpak players is like internet shopping. Instead of getting out there and doing the hard yards trying to find what you're looking for, you can just have it delivered to your door.**

*Ashley Giles, on signing overseas players rather than developing local youngsters*

**I reckon you can't pull a muscle if you haven't got any.**

*John Emburey*

**My team told me that they have yet to meet a better human being than me. This is a huge compliment.**

*Kolkata franchise owner Shah Rukh Khan succumbing to flattery*

**Buy a church and pray.**
*Geoff Boycott's tactics ahead of the second Test against New Zealand*

**At the moment they are running singles between them. Both are running half a run.**
*Harsha Bhogle assessing Virender Sehwag and Virat Kohli's running between the wickets*

**Go on Hedley, you've got him in two minds, he doesn't know whether to hit you for four or six.**
*Arthur Wood to spin bowler Hedley Verity*

**The one thing you know about Pakistan is that you have no idea what they will do**
*Ian Chappell*

**The only thing that went well for us was the warm-up before the game.**
*MS Dhoni takes the positives from an appalling show against Sri Lanka*

**It must be some measure of the catastrophic decline in Australian cricket that there are blokes in the squad these days who have not even published an autobiography, let alone a barbecue cookbook.**
*John Huxley, in the Sydney Morning Herald*

**Collingwood, with respect, is a poor man's Mark Ealham.**
*Alec Stewart*

# THE MORAL GAME

**English cricket has become Stanford's WAG.**
*Michael Atherton*

**The only time an Australian ever walks is when his car runs out of petrol.**
*Barry Richards*

**When Justin Langer finds his off stump akimbo he leaves the crease only after asking the met office whether any earthquakes have been recorded in the region. In any case, he never edges the ball. It's just that his bat handle keeps breaking.**
*Peter Roebuck*

**Cricket is a game full of forlorn hopes and sudden dramatic changes of fortune and its rules are so ill-defined that their interpretation is partly an ethical business.**
*George Orwell*

**Cricket is not a very big sport in prison**
*Allen Stanford, cricket promoter and sponsor currently serving a 110 year sentence*

**It is like giving a machine gun to a monkey. It can be fantastic, or it can be an absolute disaster too**
*Hugh Morris on players using Twitter*

**I see His Highness is a conscientious objector.**
*Douglas Jardine to the Nawab of Pataudi who refused to cooperae with the Bodyline tactics*

**They came to see me bat not you bowl.**
*WG Grace, putting the bails back on his stumps after being bowled first ball.*

**Where are you going Doctor? There's still one stump standing.**
*Charles Kortright on dismissing WG Grace*

**I don't know an England player who could fix a light bulb, let alone a match.**
*Darren Gough*

**I have seen fewer hookers in Soho on a Saturday night.**
*Bob Willis remarks on England's batting against the short ball*

**I don't suppose I can call you a lucky bleeder when you have got 347.**
*Angus Fraser on beating Brian Lara's bat in 1994*

**Ladies playing cricket? Absurd. Just like a man trying to knit.**
*Len Hutton*

**Cricket is like sex films. They both relieve frustration and tension.**
*Linda Lovelace*

**He's the hooker in a team full of virgins; the drinker in a team full of people who don't drink.**
*Mike Atherton on Andrew Symonds' situation*

**Cricket is a game which the British, not being a very spiritual people, had to invent to have some concept of eternity.**
*Lord Maycroft*

**Personally, I have always looked upon cricket as organised loafing.**
*William Temple, who was Archbishop of Canterbury*

**I'll tell you what pressure is. Pressure is a Messerschmitt up your arse. Playing cricket is not.**
*Keith Miller (who saw active service in the RAAF in WW2) to Michael Parkinson*

**Individuals are birds of passage while institutions are forever**

*India's Supreme Court on N Srinivasan and the BCCI*

**You convicts are all the same.**

*Malcolm Marshall to Steve Waugh after he refused to walk*

**You have to clap yourself on at the WACA.**

*Gary Gilmour, New South Wales all rounder*

**Don't you know who I am? I'm New Zealand cricket.**

*Jesse Ryder's modest appraisal to A&E staff when he arrived following a bar incident in Christchurch*

**We didn't have anti-perspirants back then.**

*Sunil Gavaskar explains the lack of team huddles back in the day*

**I'll put that in the same category as the third new ball. Overrated. Huddles are overrated.**

*Mark Taylor*

**Skinny white men with glasses shouldn't do Hakas.**

*Daniel Vettori explains why he doesn't do the Haka*

**I wonder who is hydrating the substitute fielders?**

*Sanjay Manjrekar raises a question about the number of substitute fielders bringing on drinks in Brisbane, during the India-Sri Lanka game*

**No matter what sort of day you've had out there today,' I'll tell them, 'I've had a worse one. I promise.'**

*Chris Scott, head coach of Cambridge MCCU, likes to remind his charges of when he dropped Lara on 18 only for him to go on and make 501*

**Getting up in the morning and putting on a pair of underpants is important for me. And I think a lot of people think like that.**

*Shane Warne hawking his new underwear range*

**Pakistan is the sort of place every man should send his mother-in-law, for a month, with all expenses paid.**

*Ian Botham*

# Technical Issues

**A pro is someone who can do great work when he doesn't feel like it.**
*Alastair Cook*

**Find out where the ball is. Go there. Hit it.**
*KJ Ranjitsinhji*

**I am a big believer that the coach is something you travel in to get to and from the game.**
*Shane Warne*

**His bat has as many holes in it as a Henry Moore sculpture.**
*John Arlott*

**Mate, if you just turn the bat over, you'll find instructions on the other side.**
*Merv Hughes to Robin Smith*

**He played a cut so late as to be positively posthumous.**
*John Arlott*

**Facing a fast bowler is like standing in the outside lane of the M1, and when the car is 22 yards away, trying to get out the way.**
*Alec Stewart*

**A natural mistimer of a ball.**
*Angus Fraser assessment of Mike Atherton*

**What do I think of the reverse sweep? It's like Manchester United getting a penalty and Bryan Robson taking it with his head.**
*David Lloyd*

**The enigma with no variation.**
*Vic Marks on Chris Lewis*

**I can hit a golf ball a long way but for some reason I struggle to hit a cricket ball a long way.**
*Alastair Cook*

**They weren't so much dives; it rather looked like he was falling off a bar stool.**
*Angus Fraser on Owais Shah's outfielding*

**His throw went absolutely nowhere near where it was going.**
*Richie Benaud*

**I need to be a little more patient at this level, and that is something I would like to improve on as fast as possible.**

*Amit Jaggernauth, West Indies' offspinner, is impatient to be patient*

**If we could stop people smoking weed we would have triple the amount of players available.**

*Lionel Cann of Bermuda on their selection problems*

**I suppose doing a love scene with Raquel Welch roughly corresponds with scoring a century before lunch.**

*Oliver Reed*

**I don't know, lad. It's unplayable at my end, but they're bowling bloody rubbish to you.**

*Brian Close to Peter Roebuck*

**I just want to get into the middle and get the right sort of runs.**

*Robin Smith, suffering from diarrhoea during an England tour of India*

**I don't think we choked this time. We never played well enough to choke.**

*Craig Matthews*

**My main aim as far as practice went was to turn up on time in order to avoid another fine from the management.**
*Phil Tufnell*

**Monty didn't understand what the coaches said. I didn't listen to them, that's why we won games for England.**
*Graeme Swann, not a great advocate of the spin coaches*

**He's not a man, in general, over afflicted with patience.**
*John Arlott commenting on Rohan Kanhai*

**I still have butterflies, but now I have them flying in formation.**
*Mark Taylor during a bad run of form*

**A fag, a cough, a cup of coffee.**
*Brian Statham describing his warm up routine*

**I suffered one or two defects ... I wasn't good enough.**
*Former prime minister John Major on his abilities as a cricketer*

**Strangely, in slow motion replay, the ball seemed to hang in the air even longer.**
*David Acfield*

**It was a hammer blow when he sacked me.**
*Alastair Cook about being sacked by James Anderson as his batting mentor after a poor run of form*

**I once delivered a simple ball, which I was told, had it gone far enough, would have been considered a wide.**
*Lewis Carroll*

**Kid yourself it's Sunday, Rev, and keep your hands together.**
*Fred Trueman, after the Revd. David Sheppard, the future Bishop of Liverpool, dropped a number of catches*

**England's always expecting. No wonder they call her the Mother Country.**
*Fred Trueman*

**You can't smoke 20 a day and bowl fast.**
*Phil Tufnell*

**I thought they were only allowed two bouncers in one over.**
*Bill Frindall, discussing a female streaker*

**Norman Cowans should remember what happened to Graham Dilley, who started off as a genuinely quick bowler. Then, they started stuffing line and length into his ear, and now he has Dennis Lillee's action with Denis Thatcher's pace.**
*Geoff Boycott*

**No good hitting me there, mate, there's nothing to damage.**
*Derek Randall to Dennis Lillee after being hit on the head by a bouncer*

**If you make a team with all the No.11s of all the teams, Hirwani would still come at No.11 in the line up.**
*Harsha Bhogle*

**I certainly did not. What sort of Nancy stuff is that?**
*Geoff Boycott on whether he touched gloves back in the day*

**I think Hawk-Eye must have had a late night.**
*Ian Botham believes Hawk-Eye got one wrong*

**He'll kill me for saying this, but he could take the lead in a musical. He has a fantastic presence on stage and he's a big man, but when he's dancing, he glides.**
*Arlene Phillips, Strictly Come Dancing judge, assessing Darren Gough's technique*

**And when John Buchanan was in charge ... let me tell you, we needed as much common sense around as we could, because I believe the coach had none.**
*Shane Warne*

**He'll bring something to the table. Cluedo, perhaps.**
*Shane Warne on John Buchanan again*

**I hope now we don't go too far the other way and lose all our drive... and try and play like New Zealand.**
*Matthew Wade is not an admirer of New Zealand cricket*

**I am the only guy there with some hair on my chest. Unfortunately, the rest of my team are all metrosexuals.**

*Simon Katich after studying the 2009 Men of Cricket calendar*

## Getting Personal

**The Spirit of Cricket demands interpretation, which in turn renders it worthless. One man's sledge is another's aside.**
*Mike Atherton*

**He's big and raw boned and I suspect he has the IQ of an empty swimming pool.**
*Adam Parore assessing Andre Nel*

**Leave our flies alone, Jardine. They're the only flamin' friends you got here.**
*An Australian supporter to Douglas Jardine*

**Tuffnell, can I borrow your brain I am building an idiot.**
*Another Australian supporter*

**Shane Warne is thicker than a complete set of Wisden year books.**
*Matt Price*

**The first time I ever met him he was the same little obnoxious weed that he is now.**
*Matthew Hayden discussing Harbhajan*

**I simply don't know how they have got to their age without electrocuting themselves or doing themselves some real harm...Rob Key asked Adil Rashid the other day what animal a lamb came from. He thought it was a cow.**

*Graeme Swann is not very impressed with his England colleagues*

**When you've been abused as many times as I have, mate, you are bound to understand some Hindi and Urdu.**

*Greg Chappell explaining his language skills*

**I am sick of political correctness. Someone asked Hayden what he thought of Harbhajan and he gave his view. Aren't you allowed to give an opinion anymore?**

*Jeff Thomson after Hayden was reprimanded for the 'obnoxious weed' comment*

**Are you aware, sir, that the last time I saw anything like that on a top lip, the whole herd had to be destroyed?**

*Eric Morecambe to Dennis Lillee*

**Can't really be an honours board if you have got Styris' name on it.**
*Ian Smith reading the names on the Hamilton honours board*

**There must be two Justin Langers in the world, I think.**
*Ricky Ponting disbelieving that Justin Langer wants sledging stopped in county cricket*

**The mincing run-up resembles someone in high heels and a panty girdle chasing after a bus.**
*Martin Johnson commenting on Merv Hughes*

**His sledging was always more subtle and intelligent than my basic stuff. It would often take me three overs to work out what he meant.**
*Merv Hughes on Mike Atherton*

**Gatting at fine leg. That's a contradiction in terms.**
*Richie Benaud*

**The candles cost more than the cake.**
*Navot Sidhu commenting on Geoffrey Boycott's age on his birthday*

**Shane Warne's idea of a balanced diet is a cheeseburger in each hand.**
**Ian Healy**
**Go and deflate yourself, you balloon.**
*Daryll Cullinan to Shane Warne*

**The O might be in front of your name now son but have a look where it is on the way back.**
*Yabba (a well-known supporter in the 1920s and 30s from Sydney) to Bill O'Reilly as he walked to the crease*

**Whoa there! He's bolted**
*Yabba to Charles Kellaway after he finally got off the mark*

**Put a penny in him, George, he's stopped registering.**
*Yabba to umpire George Borwick, who read gas meters for a living, when the Nawab of Pataudi was scoring slowly*

**Call nurse Mitchell (a notorious abortionist in those times) to get the bastard out.**
*Yabba during a stoic batting performance*

**I've seen better batters in my fridge.**
*Steve Kirby's mysterious send off to Mike Atherton*

**He's got a reputation for being awkward and arrogant, probably because he is awkward and arrogant.**
*Frances Edmonds lifts the lid on husband Phil*

**If I were being polite, I'd say that Gatt is a little long in the tooth, somewhat immobile and carries too much weight. But I prefer straight talking, so I am saying what I really think. Gatt is too old, too slow and too fat.**
*Geoff Boycott's assessment of Gatting's selection for the 1994/5 Ashes*

**How anyone can spin a ball the width of [Mike] Gatting boggles the mind.**
*Martin Johnson on Shane Warne's 'Ball of the Century'*

**If there is an uglier top three in the world than Andrew Strauss, Cook and Trott, I don't know of it.**
*Graeme Swann*

**His claim of being an all-rounder is clearly more a reflection of his physique than abilities in Test cricket.**
*Bangladesh newspaper view of captain Khaled Mahmud*

**The only change England would propose might be to replace Derek Pringle, who remains troubled by no balls.**
*The Times*

**If his batting was as good as Don Bradman's, he couldn't score enough runs to make up for what he costs them with his keeping.**
*Ian Chappell is not a fan of Kamran Akmal's wicket keeping*

**Ah yes, sledging in the days before the microphones on the pitch. We got that blind MP chap up into the commentary box to lip read.**
*Brian Johnston*

**If this letter reaches you then the Post Office thinks more of you than I do.**
*From a letter sent to Mike Denness after the disastrous 1974/5 Australian tour*

**Angus Fraser's bowling is like shooting down F-16 aeroplanes with sling shots. Even if they hit, no damage would be done. Like an old horse, he should be put out to pasture.**
*Colin Croft*

**And Glenn McGrath dismissed for two, just 98 runs short of his century.**
*Richie Benaud*

**Bruce Reid is not the worst batsman there is at international level but those who are worse would not need to hire the Myer Music Bowl to hold a convention.**
*Richie Benaud*

**Don't bother son, you won't be out there long enough.**
*Fred Trueman to an Australian batsman as he was closing the gate on entering the pitch*

**I don't think you have to say much if they are 45 all out.**
*Vernon Philander on why South Africa had not been sledging in the first Test against New Zealand in Cape Town*

**Well, Andrew Strauss is certainly an optimist – he's come out wearing sun block.**
*Australian commentator during a 5 – 0 whitewash in Australia*

**Aussie sledging? I'm just glad they've heard of me.**
*Monty Panesar*

**I don't know why he (Shane Warne) hates me. Maybe it is because my face is real and his is not.**
*Marlon Samuels*

**It's very sad when good wine goes sour.**
*Duncan Fletcher responding to Gavaskar's criticism of the England team*

**Ken Barrington: Let's cut out some quick singles**
**Fred Titmus: OK Ken, we'll cut out yours**

**David Gower: Do you want Gatt a foot wider?**
**Chris Cowdrey: No, he'd burst**

**Shane Warne: I have been waiting two years to further humiliate you.**
**Daryl Cullinan: Looks like you spent it eating**

**Simon Mann; You must have put a few people to sleep in your time, Geoffrey.**
**Geoff Boycott: Yes, but I was still batting when they woke up**

**Interviewer: Darryl, who are your favourite actors?**
**Daryl Cullinan: Dustin Hoffman and some Aussie bowlers in the act of appealing**

**Rod Marsh: How's your wife and my kids?**
**Ian Botham: The wife's fine but the kids are retarded**

**Mark Waugh: Mate, what are you doing out here. There's no way you're good enough to play for England**
**James Ormond: Maybe not, but at least I am the best player in my family**

# The Batsman

**The hardest part of the whole affair was that it took me a month to get the fake tan off.**

*Simon Katich on his disagreement with Michael Clarke in which he grabbed him round the throat*

**A bank clerk going to war.**

*The Sun's description of David Steele*

**A corpse with pads on.**

*Journalist Ian Wooldridge's description of Bill Lawry*

**The viewers have got no interest in what I've got to say because they switched off four or five hours ago.**

*Kevin Pietersen is not impressed with the slow and low Nagpur pitch, which yielded 199 for 5 in 97 overs on the first day*

**He loves the pink day. He always comes out as best dressed.**

*AB de Villiers on Faf du Plessis playing his 100th ODI in pink*

**Derek Randall bats like an octopus with piles.**

*Matthew Engel, journalist*

**Michael Atherton is one of the few people capable of looking more dishevelled at the start of a six-hour century than at the end of it.**
*Martin Johnson*

**Colin Milburn is as untidy as an unmade bed, as devastating as a hand grenade.**
*Clive Taylor, cricket correspondent of the Sun*

**Sachin Tendulkar is in my time the best player without doubt - daylight second, Brian Lara third.**
*Shane Warne*

**Dear Mum, things are looking up. Today I got a half volley in the nets.**
*David Lloyd during the 1974 – 75 tour to Australia against Lillee ad Thompson*

**Pietersen would be deemed brash by a Texan assertiveness coach.**
*Simon Wilde, Sunday Times cricket correspondent*

**His (Pietersen's) relationship with English cricket has been like an illicit affair. Full of thrills and excitement but destined to end in tears.**
*Andrew Strauss*

**Peter Siddle's first Test wicket.**
*Peter Siddle on being asked to describe Tendulkar*

**I was destined to be one of the world's greatest batsmen, but nobody other than me realised that. I'm the Tendulkar of England**
*Lord Jeffrey Archer*

**It kind of felt like I was the library in a theme park.**
*Kane Williamson, on his partnership with Brendon McCullum during his 195 in 134 balls at Christchurch*

**Ian Botham was my best room-mate. I never saw him.**
*Allan Lamb*

**Hook, line and Sinclair.**
*David Lloyd on Stuart Broad bouncing out Mathew Sinclair*

**Gooch has had so many opening partners since 1979 that he must have felt at times like the Wing Commander of the Tiger Moth Squadron...A rueful greeting in the knowledge of minimal life expectancy.**
*Martin Johnson*

**Isn't that Don Bradman over there? I would like to be introduced.**
*Winston Churchill*

**Even Ray Charles would have hit that for four.**
*Jeff Dujon on Enamul Haque Junior's square-driven four being too easy*

**I hurt my thumb then obviously the mother-in-law died.**
*Mike Gatting*

**The only person who would call for a run and wish his partner good luck at the same time.**
*John Warr appraising Dennis Compton's running between the wickets*

**You were out first ball, run out in the next innings and now you have been shot. What a terrible, terrible first tour.**
*Kumar Sangakkara on Tharanga Paranavitana's debut series, in Pakistan in 2009 during which he was attacked and badly injured*

**I am jealous of my parents. I will never have a kid as cool as them.**
*Chris Gayle*

**When he turned up, I thought, "brilliant, we've got a mascot to take on tour with us", because he looked about 16 at a push.**
*Graeme Swann remembers when a young looking Joe Root joined the England squad*

**My diet was sausages then, in no particular order, sausages, chips, sausages, toast, sausages, beans, sausages, cheese, sausages, eggs, and the occasional sausage.**
*Marcus Trescothick explains how he acquired his nickname of Banger*

**If a three-year-old is bowling me out, it's time to move over.**
*Michael Vaughan concerned his son Archie knocked out his off stump in the garden*

**I've had one offer of a job - from Lee Westwood to carry his bag.**
*Michael Vaughan discusses post retirement employment*

**If it had been a cheese roll, it would never have got past him.**
*Graham Gooch on Gatting playing 'The ball of the century'*

**It couldn't have been Gatt. Anything he takes up to his room after nine o'clock, he eats.**
*Ian Botham providing an alibi in the Gatting bar maid scandal*

**A lot depends on what they need. If they need an opener, then I'll go ahead, if it's a No. 3, then maybe Owais [Shah], if they need someone to bowl a little bit, maybe Ravi [Bopara] ... If they need an old bloke they've got Ramps.**
*Robert Key assessing the opposition for an England spot*

**It was a bit confusing with the tickets - they all said Hamilton on them, so I kept picking up everyone else's thinking it was mine.**
*Hamilton Masakadza on travelling to Hamilton, Bermuda*

**The first rule of batting is to use your bat.**
*Faf du Plessis, having twice left the ball at the Oval with unfortunate effect*

**I'd like to say it's hard to miss, but I won't**
*Chris Rogers on being hit in the box by Ishant Sharma in the first over of the Boxing Day Test at the MCG*

**WG Grace, Don Bradman, Shane Warne ... and now me.**

*Claire Taylor delight at being one of Wisden's five Cricketer's of the Year*

## The Ground

**It's typical of English cricket. A tree gets in the way for 200 years and when it falls down, instead of cheering, they plant a new one.**
*Dave Gilbert, the Australian coach, baffled by English sentimentality*

**The new Old Trafford stand is quite frankly worse than eating sprouts dipped in marmite. Washed down with turps.**
*Graeme Swann appreciating Old Trafford*

**It is named after him because the seats are wider.**
*Andrew Caddick explaining why Marcus Trescothick has a stand named after him at Taunton*

**It's a beautiful day today and as I look around the ground, I can see about 30 young girls all wearing Dutch caps.**
*Jonathan Agnew*

**I hope it explodes.**
*Glenn Maxwell on being asked what he wanted from the pitch after Australia compiled 451*

**I'd describe it as a jigsaw with half the pieces missing.**
*Mike Hesson, New Zealand cricket coach, on the pitch at Blacktown after the New Zealand warm-up game was abandoned due to safety concerns*

**It looks more suitable for growing carrots.**
*Andy Atkinson, ICC grounds inspector assessing Bermuda's new pitch*

**Wickets are like wives - you never know which way they will turn.**
*Navjot Singh Sidhu*

**Yes, because both sides have such bad batsmen. That's my honest opinion, they're useless.**
*Phil Stoyanoff, the Napier grounds man, on why he thought it a result pitch*

**England trained and grass grew at the MCG yesterday, two activities virtually indistinguishable from each other in terms of tempo.**
*Greg Baum, Australian sports journalist*

**That sums up the wicket. If I'm getting runs on it.**
*Ryan Harris on the MCG pitch*

**You join us at a very appropriate time. Ray Illingworth has just relieved himself at the Pavilion End.**
*Brian Johnston*

**It is a full house in Eden Gardens. Today, Calcutta is celebrating the assassination of Mahatma Gandhi.**
*Brian Johnston*

**This MCG wicket has more bounce than a Baywatch beach sprint.**
*Damien Fleming daydreaming on ABC radio*

**There is no limit to what England cricketers can achieve, as long as you keep them off the pitch.**
*Giles Smith, Times journalist*

**It should start doing a bit by day seven.**
*Evan Flint, the Newlands grounds man assesses the pitch after Sri Lanka decided to field*

**At 80 years of age, he (the Eden Gardens grounds man) has got more life than this pitch.**
*Jeff Dujon is not a fan of the pitch at Eden Gardens*

**The captains... say it's a batting wicket, bowlers have no chance. They don't have the bowlers to have a chance**

*Anurudda Polonowita, Sri Lanka's groundsman, has explains a boring high scoring draw*

**The smell on the outfield was diabolical, and it was obviously stale wee ... the main worry for the fielding side was when it came to having to shine the ball.**

*Hampshire's wicketkeeper, Nic Pothas, on the Old Trafford ground after an Artic Monkeys concert. A lack of latrine facilities seems to have caused a problem*

## The Bowler

**Eeyore without the joie de vivre.**
*Mike Selvey's assessment of Angus Fraser*

**It was like watching Edward Scissorhands coping with a cricket ball coming down at him from a great height.**
*Monty Panesar describes his catching technique*

**I look like I do on the field because what I do is knackering.**
*Angus Fraser*

**The best ball I've bowled – I've wasted it on Chris Martin, no offence Chris**
*Nathan Lyon remembers a wonder ball to one of the worst number 11s*

**The face of a choirboy, the demeanor of a civil servant and the ruthlessness of a rat catcher.**
*Geoff Boycott describing Derek Underwood*

**A 1914 biplane tied up with elastic bands vainly trying to take off.**
*Frank Keating describing Bob Willis' run up*

**There are 10,000 people in that stadium and 3,000 of them will be overweight...Freddie has become a role model for them.**
*Andrew 'Chubby' Chandler who is Flintoff's agent*

**My theory is that every time a batsman plays and misses he should be asked to take off one piece of protective clothing of the bowler's choice.**
*Michael Kasprowicz wants the Laws changed*

**There was a time when a batsman had more chance of being hit by space debris than being done in the flight by Ashley Giles.**
*Mike Selvey*

**I think I had about eight names for the one that went straight.**
*Shane Warne*

**Harris, can you turn a doorknob?**
*A placard questioning Paul Harris at Newlands.*

**Paul Harris is a buffet bowler - you just help yourself.**
*Geoff Boycott is of the same opinion*

**I'd have looked faster in colour.**
*Fred Trueman*

**I might need it, so I haven't framed it yet.**
*Darren Pattinson thinks he might add to his one cap for England before he has it framed*

**I've not seamed a ball for four months. I can't wait to bowl in England again.**
*Stuart Broad on tour in the West Indies*

**Built like Tarzan, plays like Jane.**
*Ricky Ponting on Shaun Tait*

**It was like facing the World XI at one end and Illford 2nd XI at the other.**
*Mike Gatting on facing Richard Hadlee playing for New Zealand*

**We're not good friends at all, I just pretend to get on with him because he's bloody fast and I don't want him to hurt me in the nets.**
*Paul Harris on his relationship with Dale Steyn*

**Murali will complete 1000 Test wickets but they would count as mere run outs in my eyes.**
*Bishan Bedi view Muttiah Muralitharan's bowling style*

**England's pace bowlers are making the helmet go out of fashion.**
*Scyld Berry*

**Merv Hughes always appeared to be wearing a tumble-dried ferret on his top lip.**
*Rick Broadbent, sportswriter at The Times*

**This bowler's like my dog, three short legs and balls that swing each way.**
*Brian Johnston*

**If a cigarette butt in the bottom of a beer bottle had a voice it would be the voice of Phil Tufnell.**
*Telford Vice*

**Who can forget Malcolm Devon.**
*Ted Dexter, when Chairman of Selectors, almost remembering Devon Malcolm*

**If this bloke's a Test Match bowler, then my backside is a fire engine.**
*David Lloyd discussing Nathan Astle*

**Gym. Like dancing, holding hands, queueing. Overrated.**
*Shane Warne*

**Being Hoggard's runner would be like being Prince Edward's break-dance instructor: the pay would be fine and, like as not, you would have plenty of time to yourself.**
*Giles Smith, the Times columnist, on Alastair Cook's role as Matthew Hoggard's runner*

**The whole second innings thing is a blur. Luckily, there are highlights, so you can see it every ten minutes on television.**
*Morne Morkel clearly relishing Australia's collapse at Newlands*

**Not seen that many wickets fall in a day's play since 1996 in my back garden ... and at least that was a green seamer.**
*Stuart Broad tweets after 16 wickets went down on the first day of the third Test between Pakistan and England in Dubai*

**Freddie Flintoff said he wanted to bowl 75 overs in a Test match here (at Lord's) not because he was trying to take wickets but because he was trying to burn off all the calories, he ate over the time he spent here.**
*Andrew Whillas, the operations manager at Lord's, on the legendary Lord's meals*

**I've heard batsmen complaining, "the ball is swinging". But the ball is supposed to swing. We're not here to give only throwdowns.**
*Jasprit Bumrah*

**When Merv leaves school, he is going to have to be very good at football and cricket.**
*Merv Hughes school report*

**If James could take one thing to a deserted island he would definitely take his mirror.**
*Michael Clarke on team-mate James Pattinson*

**I'm always up for a challenge but eating a kangaroo's bits is no way to prove yourself.**
*Darren Gough is not going to do 'I'm A Celebrity Get Me Out of Here'*

**The way I look at it, at one stage Victoria had two world record holders. Shane Warne with the most Test wickets and me with the most runs.**
*Mick Lewis, who holds the record for most runs conceded in an ODI*

**Unfortunately, I was born with a straight arm**
*Ravi Shastri explaining his lack of a quicker delivery*

**Watching some of the bowlers' actions today, I think I might have created a monster.**
*Arjuna Ranatunga, former Sri Lankan captain, on the consequences of defending Muttiah Muralitharan's action*

**I was starting to stiffen up already.**
*Michael Hussey after a spell of one over in Pallekele*

**Bloody Derby. What a way to go.**
*Johnathan Agnew on his final game against Derbyshire before retirement*

# THE ADMINISTRATORS

**Pietersen has been dismissed for being a South African egomaniac. This is not news ... What next? (The ECB) will appoint a dog and sack him for going woof.**
*Simon Barnes, The Times*

**I went to the toilet to listen to it ... So I called him, sitting on the toilet, and that's how I heard I'd been picked for England.**
*Graham Onions on hearing of his Test selection*

**The ICC may well be the voice of cricket; the BCCI is an invoice.**
*Mansur Ali Khan Pataudi on the BCCI's obsession with money*

**Any sporting body which re-elects Giles Clarke unopposed as its chairman must have more screws loose than a DIY flat-pack.**
*Mike Walters of the Daily Mirror on the appointment of Giles Clarke as Chairman of the ECB*

**Cricket must be the only business where you can earn more in one day than three.**
*Pat Gibson*

**I am amused to see Colin Graves described as a no nonsense Yorkshireman. Ever since he was appointed it has been nothing but nonsense.**
*Henry Blofeld*

**The ICC ... are in meltdown. This is an organisation with all the brains of a chocolate mouse.**
*Geoff Boycott*

**The Kiwis will be very upset.**
*Sanjay Manjrekar after the programming director got the flags of Australia and New Zealand mixed up*

**Feed him to the Alsatians ... then he won't come back.**
*Geoffrey Boycott on how the authorities should deal with a drunken spectator*

**You tried to start the wave and that's not allowed. We don't muck around up here.**
*A police officer to two Australia fans, Luke Cassidy and Paul Resnikoff, who were accused of trying to start a Mexican Wave at the Gabba*

# THE ASHES

**Which of you bastards called this bastard a bastard?**

*Bill Woodfull to his team after a complaint from Douglas Jardine*

**How can you call it a clash of cultures when you're playing against a country with no culture?**

*David Gower's assessment of the Ashes*

**I don't think we have met. My name's Cowdrey.**

*Colin Cowdrey, having been selected as an emergency measure aged 41, introduces himself at the crease to Jeff Thompson*

**Man for man on paper, the Australia side stand out like dog's balls.**

*Greg Chappell assessing the relative merits of the 1984 Ashes teams*

**When in Rome...**

*Michael Atherton after being accused of cheating by Ian Healey after not walking*

**He's a smashing lad - very un-Australian.**

*Chris Adams discusses Ryan Harris*

**The traditional dress of the Australian cricketer is the Baggy Green cap on the head and the chip on the shoulder.**
*Simon Barnes*

**In Australia they think I'm Stephen Hawking.**
*Andrew Flintoff after presenting a current affairs programme in Australia*

**Lillee and Thompson remain a combination to conjure with, as sinister in England as Burke and Hare, or Bismarck and Tirpitz.**
*Gideon Haigh*

**For a large part of that I thought, there is no way I get paid enough to be facing him.**
*Rob Key on the delights of batting against Mitchell Johnson*

**I haven't noticed too many comments about my Aussie background out in the middle, but that's probably because I haven't been batting long enough to notice.**
*Geraint Jones*

**McCague will go down in Test cricket history as the rat who joined the sinking ship.**

*Sydney newspaper of Australia raised Martin McCague's 1993 selection for England*

**England have only three major problems. They can't bat, they can't bowl and they can't field.**

*Martin Johnson's assessment at the start of the 1986-87 Australia report*

**Right quote: wrong team**

*Martin Johnson after England winning the Ashes in 1986-87*

**Come on Brearley, for God's sake. You make Denness look like Don Bradman.**

*An Australian supporter on the 1978-79 tour*

**A cricket tour in Australia would be the most delightful period in your life...if you were deaf.**

*Harold Larwood*

**Leaving out Dennis Lillee against England would be as unthinkable as the Huns dropping Attila.**

*Australian TV commentator*

**With the possible exception of Rolf Harris, no other Australian has inflicted more pain and grief on Englishmen since Don Bradman.**
*Daily Mirror journalist Mike Walters' assessment on the retirement of Steve Waugh*

**Bailey, I wish you were a statue, and I was a pigeon.**
*An Australian supporter to Trevor Bailey in 1953/54*

**Nearly 30 years since his only tour of Australia, mention of Tavaré still occasions winces and groans. Despite its continental lilt, his name translates into Australian as a very British brand of obduracy, that Trevor Baileyesque quality of making every ditch a last one.**
*Gideon Haigh*

**Tavaré, slim, round-shouldered, with a faint moustache, looked careworn and world-weary from the moment he graduated to international cricket.**
*Gideon Haigh*

**The last positive thing England did for cricket was invent it.**
*Ian Chappell*

**Peter Siddle popped over to Sainsbury's and got me a big bar of Dairy Milk.**
*Steve Smith on how he celebrated his double century at Old Trafford*

**Nice place Buckingham Palace. The Queen has clearly done very well for herself.**
*Matthew Hoggard after the winning 2005 team's visit to the Queen*

**We finished third in a two horse race.**
*Matt Prior on the 2013/14 Ashes*

**Aussies are big and empty, just like their country.**
*Ian Botham*

**I stayed up till 1.30 in the morning to watch him cry live on TV. What a pleasure that was.**
*Matt Prior enjoying schadenfreude of watching David Warner after the sandpaper scandal*

**Nah, just the Ashes.**
*Nathan Lyon responding to spectators who asked him if he had sandpaper in his pockets*

**It should be the Empire XI. They got any Poms in their side?**
*Allan Border*

**Greg Chappell at first slip wearing the long-sleeved jumper, wide brim hat and long sleeved t-shirt, Ian Chappell at second slip wearing a short sleeved jumper and wide brim hat and Redpath at 3rd slip wearing no jumper at all...a progressive strip tease.**
*John Arlott*

**There's a misfielding epidemic going around...and it's not catching.**
*Robin Jackman*

**Prats of the Caribbean**
*A Mirror headline on England's tour of the West Indies*

**We didn't have metaphors in our day. We didn't beat about the bush.**
*Fred Trueman*

**One day there will be a radio with pictures.**
*Max Walker*

**Jesse Ryder's favourite shot - tequila.**
*A banner at the Westpac Stadium in Wellington*

**Australia were murdered, just as we were murdered. Test in, Test out all last summer. It was like finding an old mate in the next bed in intensive care.**
*Ian Wooldridge after the Australian series against the West Indies in 1984*

**He's usually a good puller – but he couldn't get it up that time.**
*Richie Benaud*

**I don't expect Jesse to have heard of me too much. I have a reasonably intelligent audience.**
*Mark Watson, New Zealand sports commentator*

**Clinching the (County) Championship is a strange sensation... There's more atmosphere in a doctor's waiting room.**
*Simon Hughes*

**Those actions suggest that, beneath the veneer of Jesse the Lad, actually lurks Jesse the Tosser.**
*Steve Deane, in the New Zealand Herald*

**To think of New Zealand cricket is to think of an afternoon in dullsville.**
*Stephen Brenkley, journalist*

**There's only one head bigger than Tony Greig's - and that's Birkenhead.**
*Fred Trueman*

**Those are the only balls you have touched all day.**
*Yabba (Stephen Gascoigne), an Australian supporter to an English batsman adjusting his box*

**She was a lovely lady and quite ample. In fact, Muttiah Muralitharan would have had plenty of room to sign his name.**
*David Lloyd*

**Simon Hughes thanks everyone who donated to today's benefit collection, which raised 1230 pounds, 30 pence, 70 Canadian cents, 50 pesetas, 1 Kenyan shilling and 2 Iranian rials.**
*Announcement during Simon Hughes' benefit game in 1991*

**There is a hint of hypocrisy about a cricketer who affects to let his bat do the talking, then in the next breath has his talk do the baiting.**
*Gideon Haigh*

**And a sedentary seagull flies by.**
*Brian Johnston*

**Barring injuries or sexual indiscretions between now and next Thursday, the three newcomers (Barnett, Russel and Lawrence), seem certain to get the benefit of Peter May's Emporium Giant 1988 England cap sale.**

*Matthew Engel disagreeing with selection policy*

**It was an excellent performance in the field marred only when Harris dropped Crapp in the outfield.**

*BBC commentator (Crapp was the batsman)*

**In the back of Hughes' mind must be the thought that he will dance down the piss and mitch one.**

*Tony Greig*

**England have nothing to lose here, apart from the Test Match.**

*David Lloyd*

**Richie Benaud eyes the camera with the look of a disdainful lizard.**

*Brian Viner*

**There's Neil Harvey standing at leg slip with his legs wide apart, waiting for a tickle.**

*Brian Johnston*

**I don't think I have seen anything quite like that before – it's the second time it has happened today.**
*Brian Johnston*

**He didn't quite manage to get his leg over.**
*Jonathan Agnew, on Botham losing his balance onto his wicket*

**Unless something happens that we can't predict, I don't think a lot will happen.**
*Fred Trueman*

**Monty Python comes up and bowls.**
*Henry Blofeld mistaking Monty Panesar*

**Ganguly has thrown a drowning man both ends of the rope.**
*Navjot Singh Sidhu on Ganguly running Dravid out after sending him back midway*

**He's about as handy as an ashtray on a motorbike.**
*Rodney Hogg gives a view on Michael Clarke's ability*

**As he comes into bowl Titmus has got two short legs one of them square.**
*Brian Johnston*

**The bowler's Holding the batsman's Willey.**
*Brian Johnston*

**It would be unprintable on television.**
*Geoff Boycott*

**However, if you don't want to hear the truth, then don't ask him for a frank opinion. Greg grew up in a household where frank opinions were served up at breakfast more often than cereal and fruit juice.**
*Ian Chappell on brother Greg*

**I thought I'd missed a whole day of my life.**
*Mark Taylor, former Aussie captain, went to bed when South Africa were 49 for 1 at Newlands, and awoke soon after to find Australia 21 for 9*

**Like an elephant trying to do the pole vault.**
*Jonathan Agnew describing Inzamam's unsuccessful attempt to clamber over his stumps*

**On the first day Logie decided to chance his arm and it came off.**
*Trevor Bailey*

**A few years ago, England would have struggled to beat the Eskimos.**
*Ian Botham*

**One of Pietersen's great triumphs this week was that he managed to get the assortment of drunks, cynics, skivers, scoundrels, gamblers and geeks collectively known as the press corps buzzing with excitement.**
*Michael Atherton of The Times*

**This shirt is unique. There are only 200 of them.**
*Richie Benaud*

**I reckon my mum could have caught that in her pinny.**
*Geoffrey Boycott on another dropped catch.*

**Dhoni is extremely quick between the wickets and Ashwin ... Ah let's just say he has other skills**
*Harsha Bhogle*

**If he (Paul Collingwood) was playing outside your house, you'd shut the curtains.**
*David Lloyd*

**The Indian team is famous for being a collection of monstrous egos sloshing about in great vats of self-importance.**
*Alex Parker, Times columnist*

**As a preparation for a Test Match, the domestic game is the equivalent of training for the Olympic marathon by taking the dog for a walk.**
*Martin Johnson*

**It's a unique occasion – a repeat of Melbourne 1977.**
*Jim Laker*

**A Test match without Botham is like a horror film without Boris Karloff.**
*Fred Trueman*

**This is Cunis at the Vauxhall End. Cunis—a funny sort of name. Neither one thing nor the other.**
*Alan Gibson*

**Chris Read's treatment has been scandalous. I've started calling him Lord Lucan because he has disappeared off the radar inexplicably.**
*Ian Botham*

**They're not bad this lot, but if we played them on uncovered wickets, we'd give them an innings start.**

*Ray Illingworth on the Yorkshire Championship winning side of 2001*

**If there's an appealing XI, Sangakkara would be captain of that as well**

*Bob Willis*

**I was once offered a Fosters from someone over the fence, but it was warmer and frothier than a Fosters.**

*Bob Willis discussing a generous Australian supporter*

**An oyster bar - apparently it puts lead in your pencil. I don't know about that. I think it only matters if you have got someone to write to.**

*David Lloyd on being asked where he went last night*

# 20/20 CRICKET

**I do not wish Twenty20 well, though I welcome new funds for cricket and cricketers. I think Twenty20 is a decadent, dumbed-down, third-rate formula for sub-prime cricket.**

*William Rees-Mogg, former Times editor, has issues with 20/20 cricket*

**One-day cricket is an exhibition. Test cricket is an examination.**

*Henry Blofeld*

**It is in my top three.**

*New Zealand's Kane Williamson, when asked if 20/20 is his favourite format of the game*

**An IPL auction is the best physio in the world.**

*Ravi Shastri thinks the IPL auction gets players fit*

**Frankenstein's monster. Soon it'll be 10/10, 5/5, then one ball to hit a six or you're hanged. Include me out.**

*Michael Simkin, author of Fatty Batter, is not a fan of the shorter format*

**In terms of sporting endeavour and prestige, the IPL is to cricket what diarrhea is to dodgy curry houses - an unfortunate by-product.**

*Paul Lewis, in the New Zealand Herald, not a fan of the IPL*

**There was a little element of feeling like a cow.**

*Adam Gilchrist on being auctioned for US$700,000*

**They've started this filthy floodlit Cricket with cricketers wearing tin hats and advertisements for contraceptives on their boots.**

*Alan Ayckbourn*

**For a start playing for your country rather than a cement company or movie production group helps.**

*David Leggat, journalist at the New Zealand Herald, explains why the World Twenty20 was a success*

**He actually sent me a text message this morning and said, 'I can't believe you're worth double what I am'.**

*David Hussey on being auctioned for more than brother Michael in the IPL players' auction*

**This is not cricket. This is the greatest divide between the rich and the poor. With that kind of money, you could have built another cement factory.**

*Jaswant Singh, Opposition leader in India, is not a fan of the IPL*

**It must seem like volunteer work to those who have drunk from the IPL's ruby-encrusted goblet.**

*Peter Lalor, journalist*

**Violence between players? Scantily clad cheerleaders? Toss in a rant by Charles Barkley and three minutes of commercials for every 45 seconds of actual game time and cricket may finally be ready for a mainstream American audience.**

*The Los Angeles Times believes the IPL would thrive in the USA*

**Can you, I was asked by a leading television executive, imagine cricket lovers rushing down St John's Wood Road to see a franchise called Vodafone Team London owned by an ageing rock star?**

*Giles Clarke, ECB Chairman, doesn't think a city-based competition would work in England*

**Will Tests soon be marketed as 'Like Twenty20, only slower'?**
*Patrick Kidd, journalist*

**The best part was in the bar afterwards. Everybody was banned so it was a pretty relaxed atmosphere. I had a blast.**
*Shane Bond on life in the Indian Cricket League*

**We put men on the moon, so why can't we have a reserve day?**
*Steve Rhodes, Bangladesh coach, annoyed at the third washout in five days at the World Cup*

**I don't mind really ... except she really did seem to be doing her job very well when I was out. She didn't have to look so pleased.**
*Jacques Kallis on his sister Janine, a cheerleader for Chennai, celebrating his wicket*

**Virender Sehwag saved IPL by picking me.**
*Chris Gayle*

**This might take half an hour.**
*Rahul Dravid when asked to pinpoint the reasons behind India's disappointing series in England*

**My secret is very simple. The wife came to watch me today.**
*AB de Villiers after scoring 129 off 52 balls for Royal Challengers Bangalore*

**Getting a hundred in 31 balls was unheard of. I took 31 balls to get off the mark**
*Sunil Gavaskar*

**I think the 1983 team was better-looking than the 2011 team.**
*Sunil Gavaskar, on the big difference between his World Cup-winning side and the most recent winners*

**Survived most frightening drive from Chittagong hotel to the airport. The driver didn't know where his off stump was, bit like the Bangladeshi batsmen.**
*Ramiz Raja*

**I know who the favourite son is now. Dad actually said he was keen on me and I didn't even get one bid off him.**
*Shaun Marsh after father Geoff, who coaches the IPL's Pune Warriors, only bid for younger brother Mitchell at the auction*

**The game's called Twenty20, it's not called One1.**

*Daniel Vettori on super overs after getting hit for 25 by Chris Gayle*

## ONE LAST THING...

**If you have enjoyed this book I would love you to write a review of the book on Amazon. It is really useful feedback as well as giving untold encouragement to the author.**

**If you have any comments, corrections, suggestions for improvements or for other books I would love to hear from you, and you can contact me at;**

**jamesconradbooks@gmail.com**

**Your comments are greatly valued, and the books have already been revised and improved as a result of helpful suggestions from readers.**

Printed in Great Britain
by Amazon

13418269R00058